Rare Diamond Ladies

Platinum Olympia as Blonde $5.00

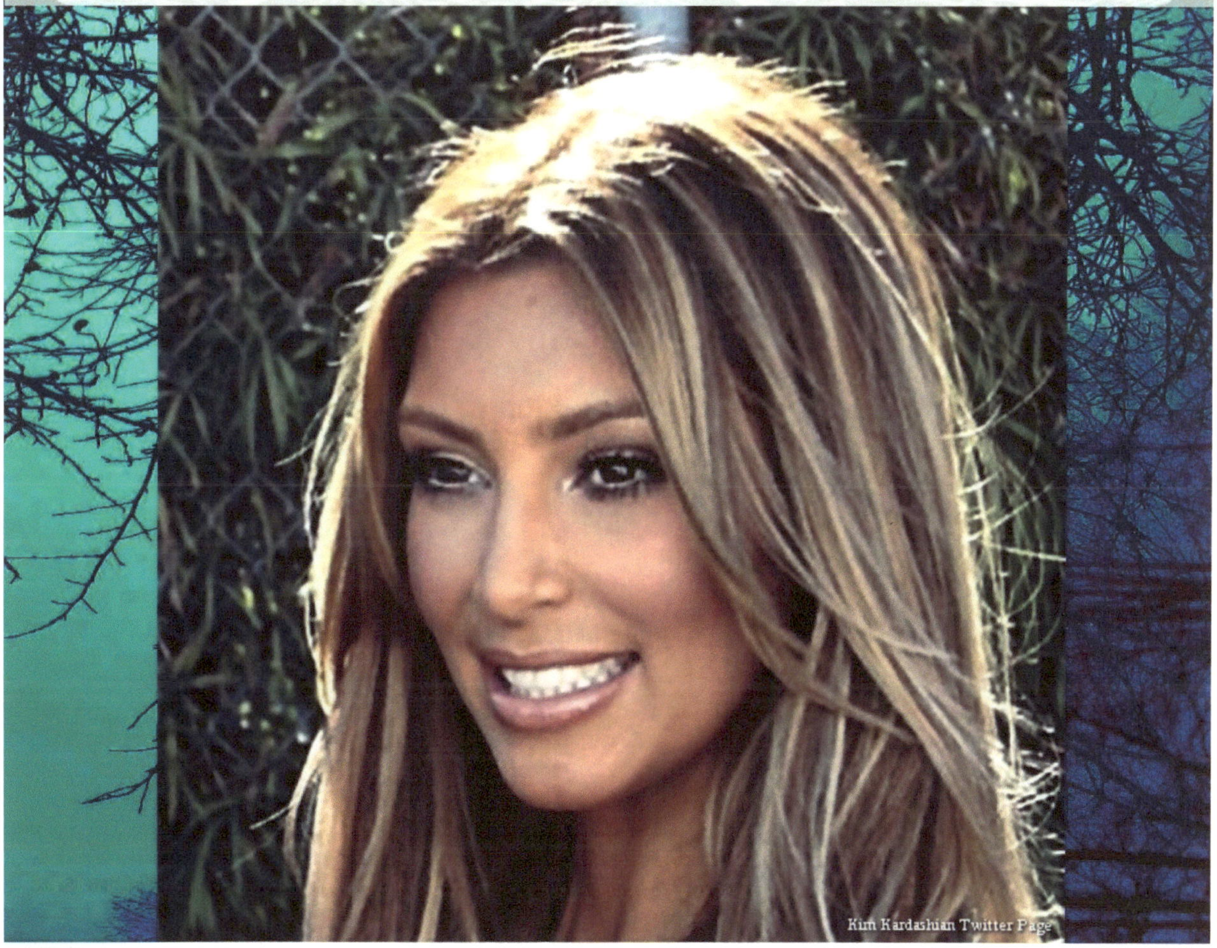

Kim Kardashian Twitter Page

Olympia Kardashian x_____2017

Dust your boots, shine like the Goddess Miss. Olympia

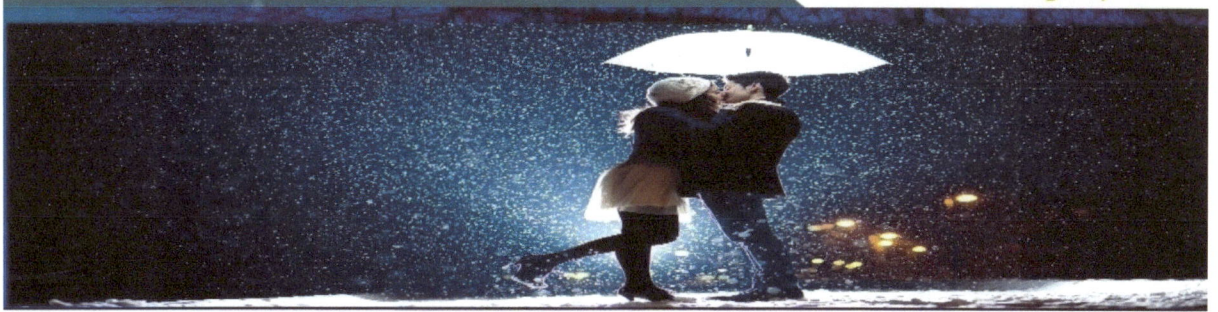

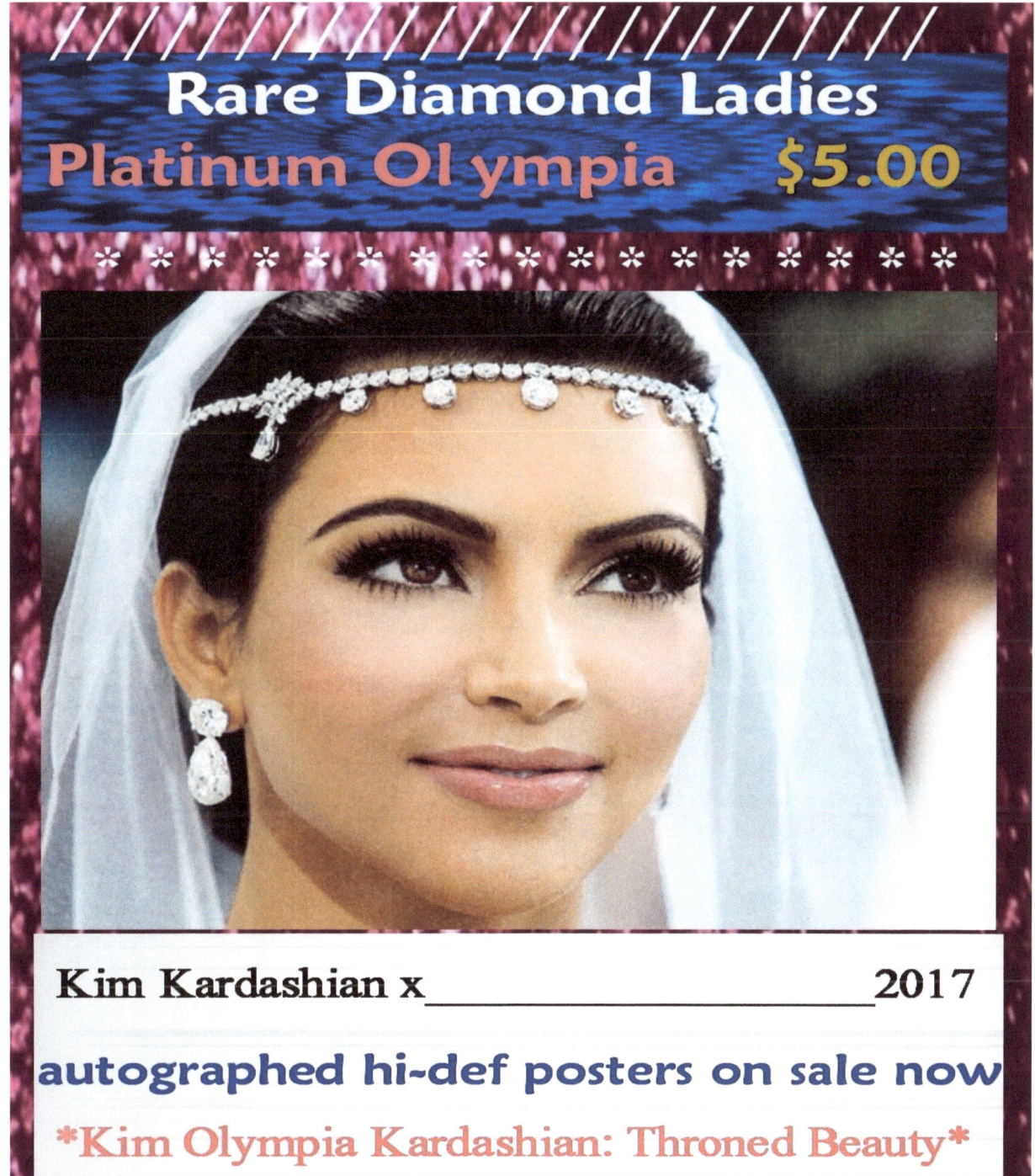

autographed hi-def posters on sale now

Kim Olympia Kardashian: Throned Beauty

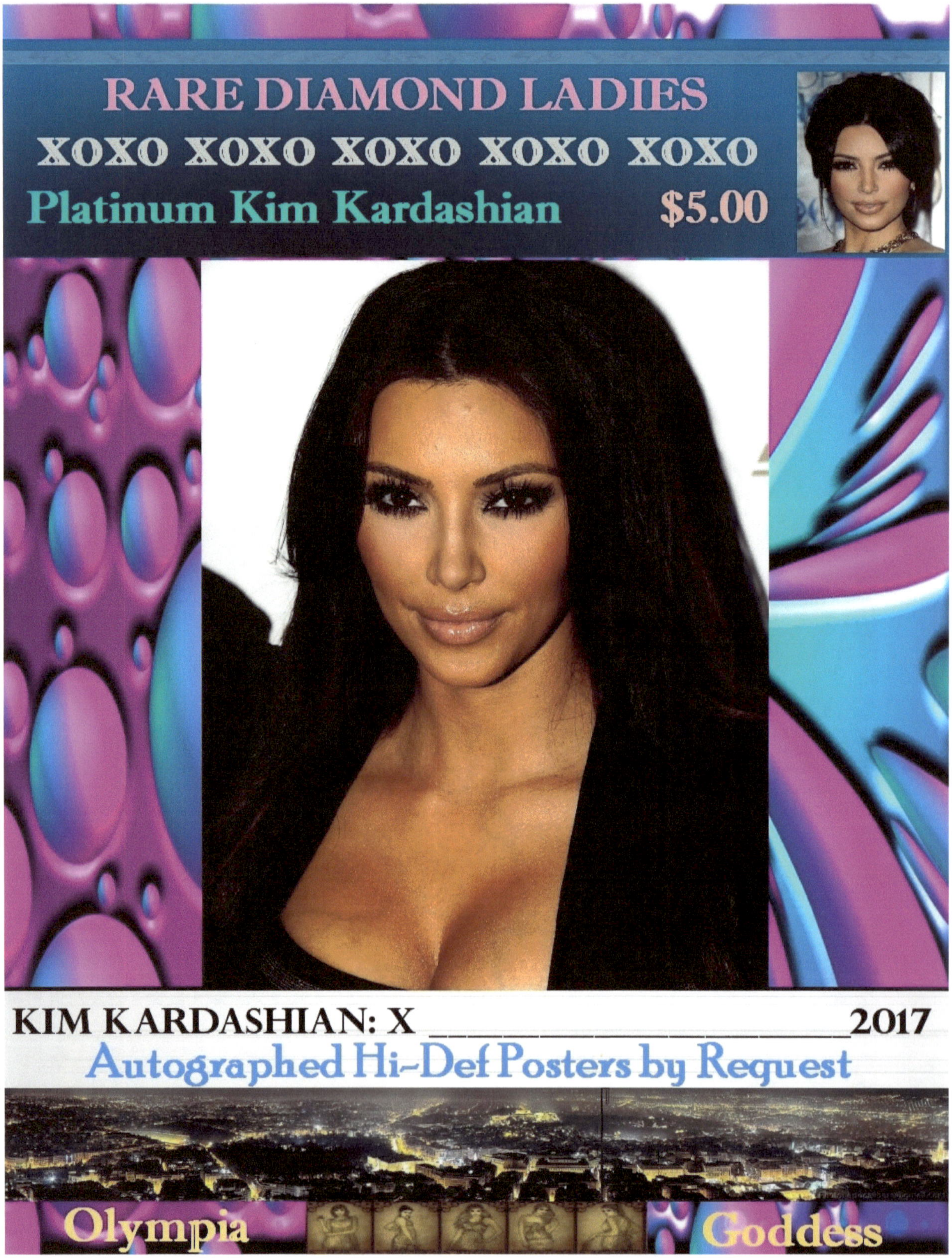

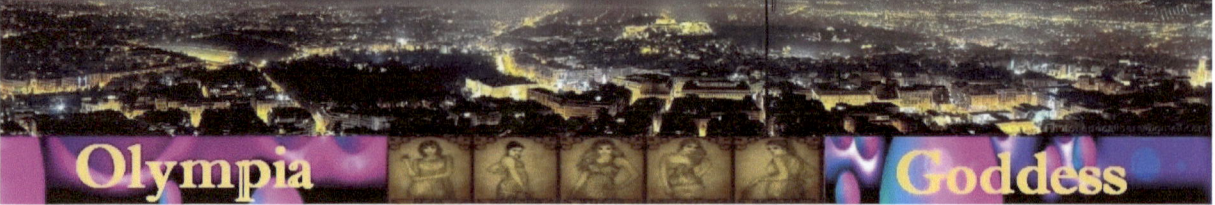

RARE DIAMOND LADIES

XOXO XOXO XOXO XOXO XOXO

Platinum Kim Kardashian $5.00

KIM KARDASHIAN: X _____ **2017**

Autographed Hi-Def Posters by Request

Olympia   Goddess

RARE DIAMOND LADIES

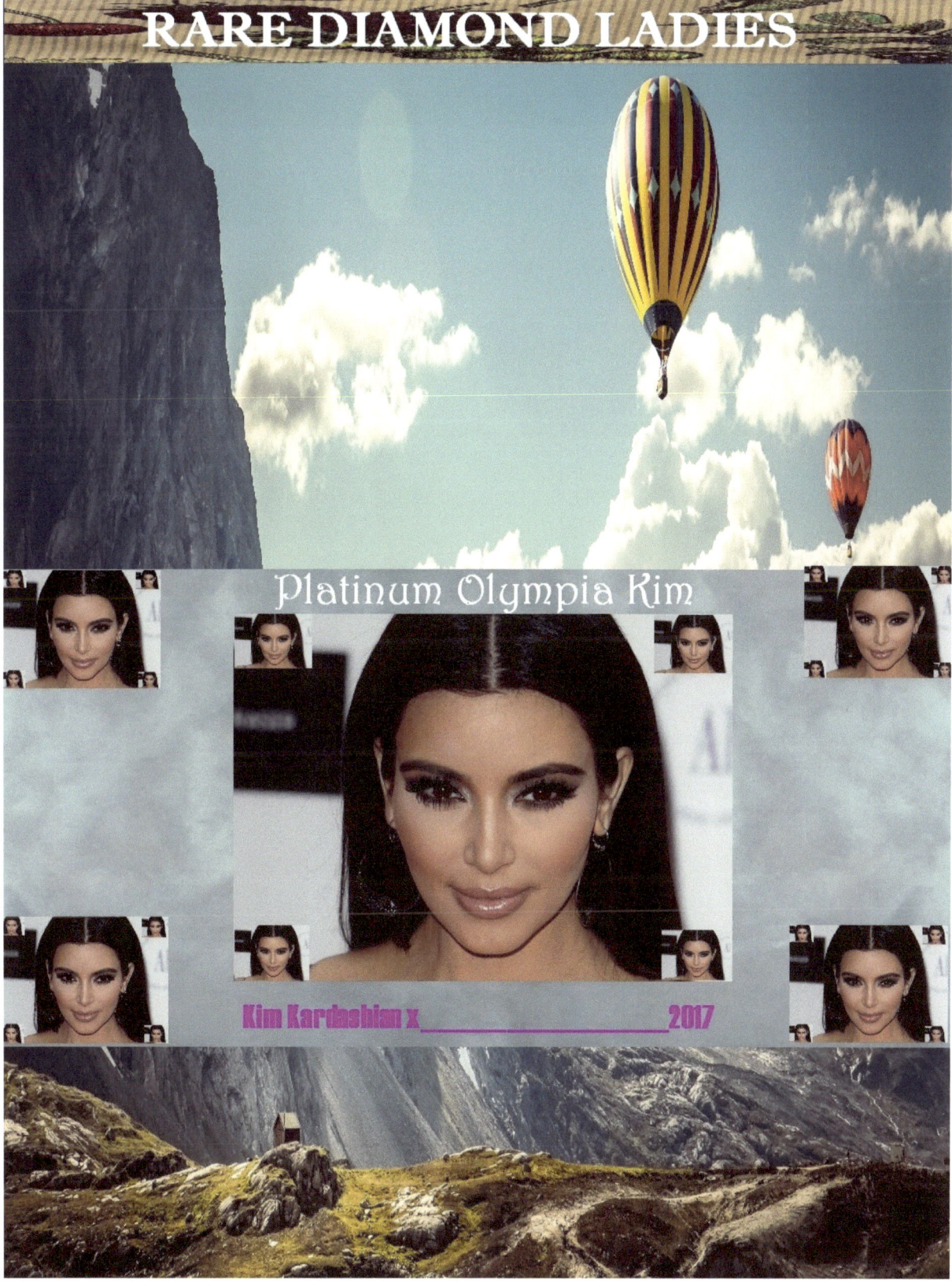

Platinum Olympia Kim

Kim Kardashian x_____2017

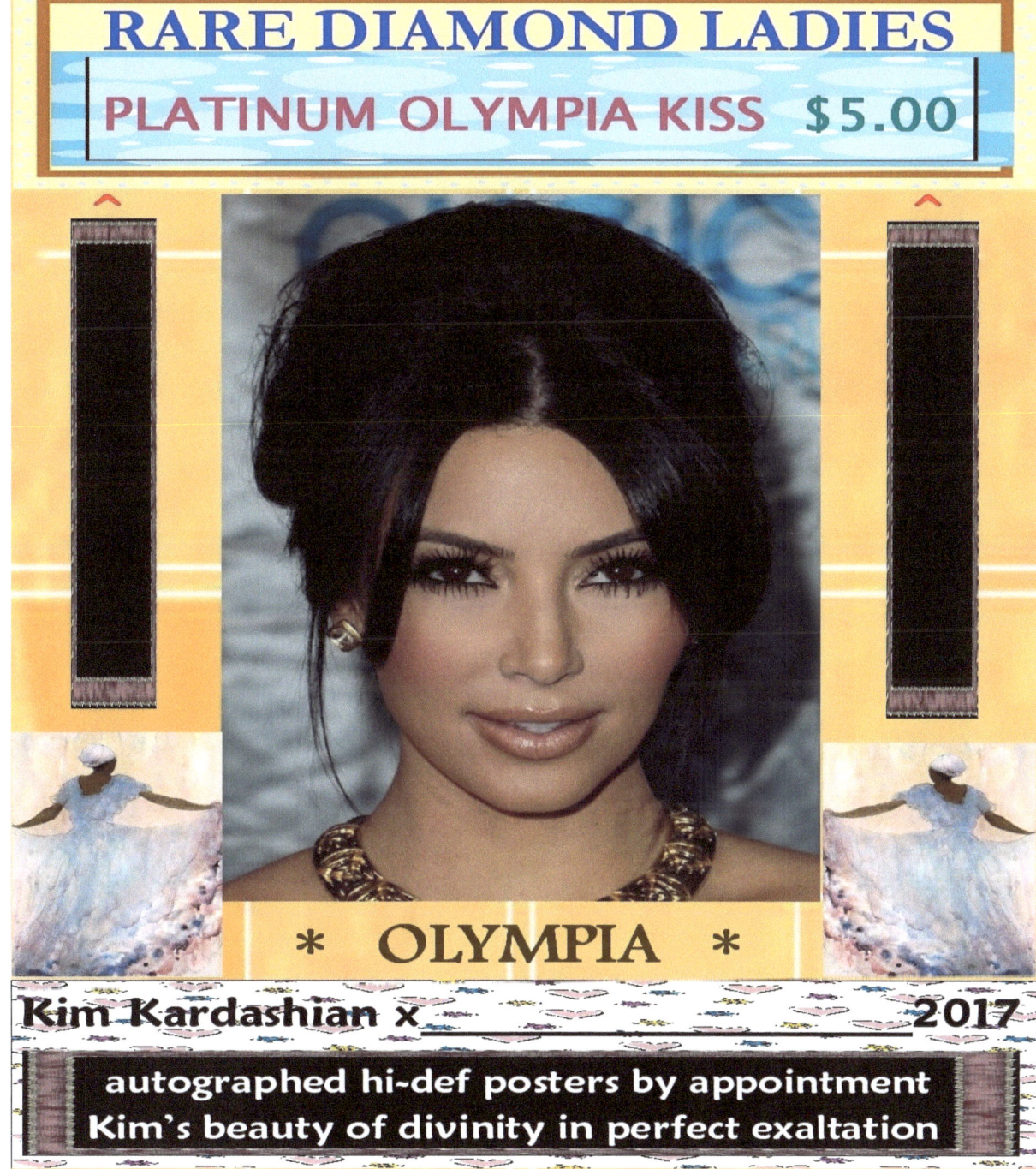

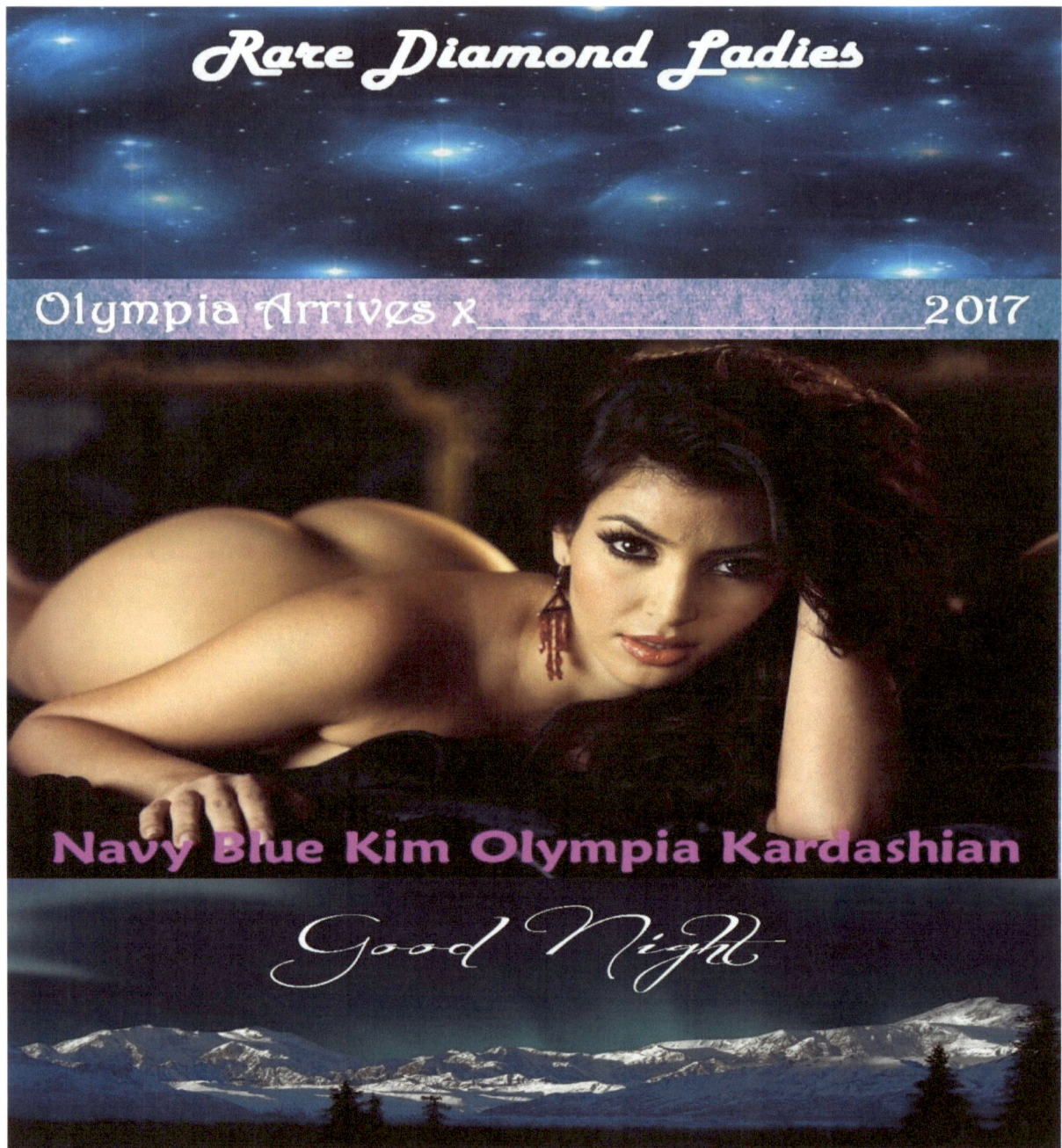

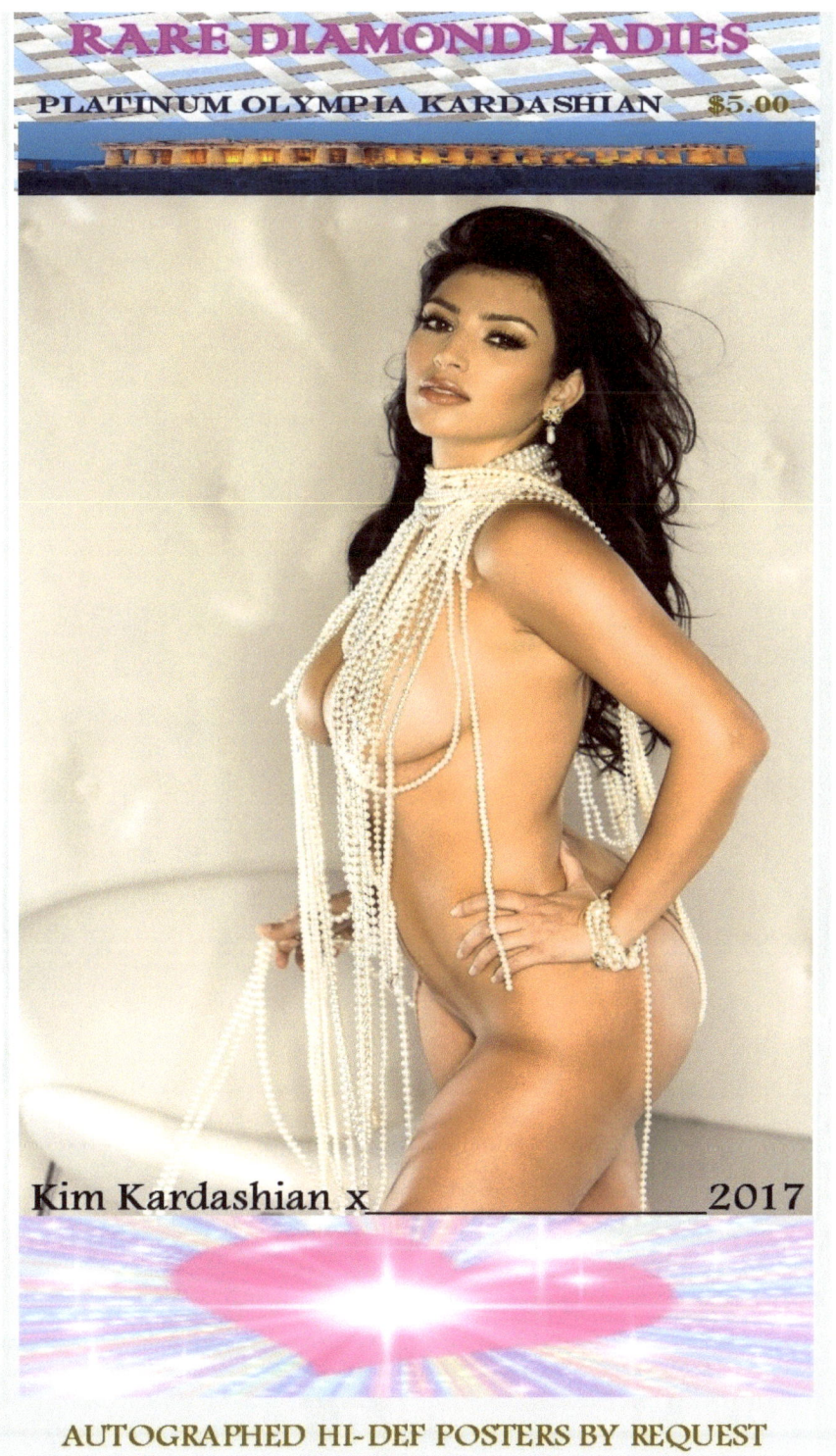

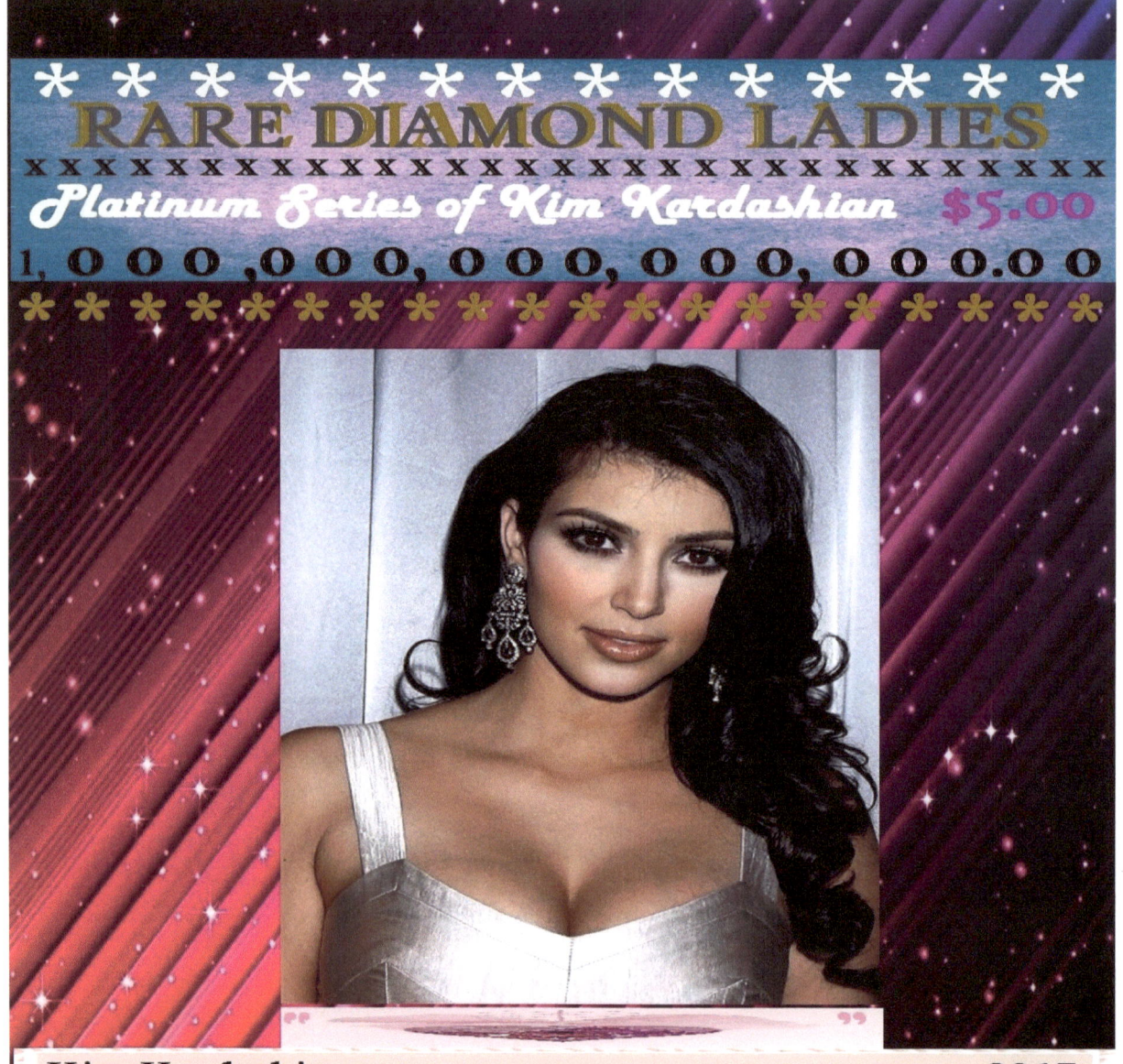

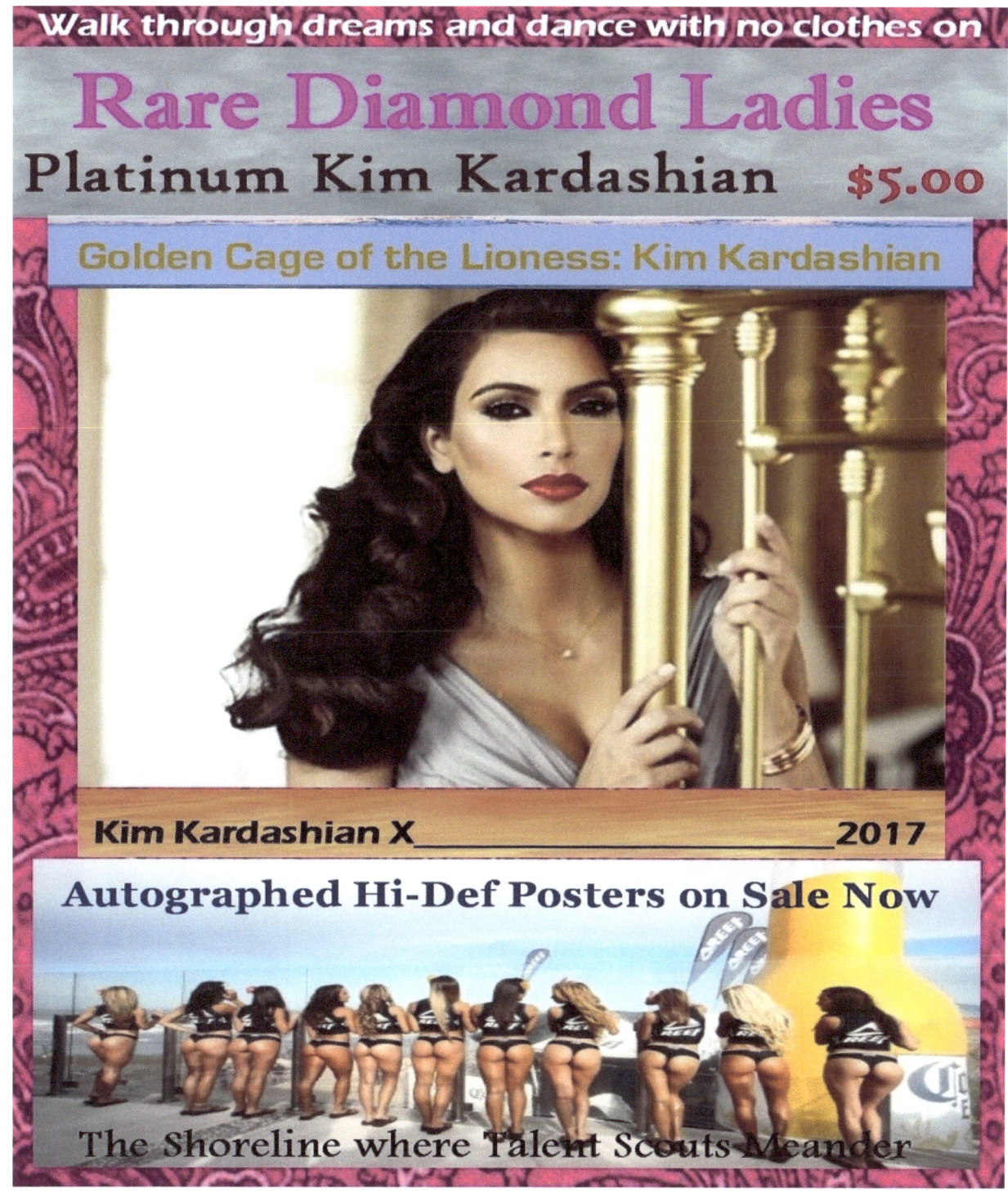

* RARE DIAMOND LADIES *

$1,000,000,000,000,000,000,000,000,000.00

Goddess: Olympia Kardashian $10.

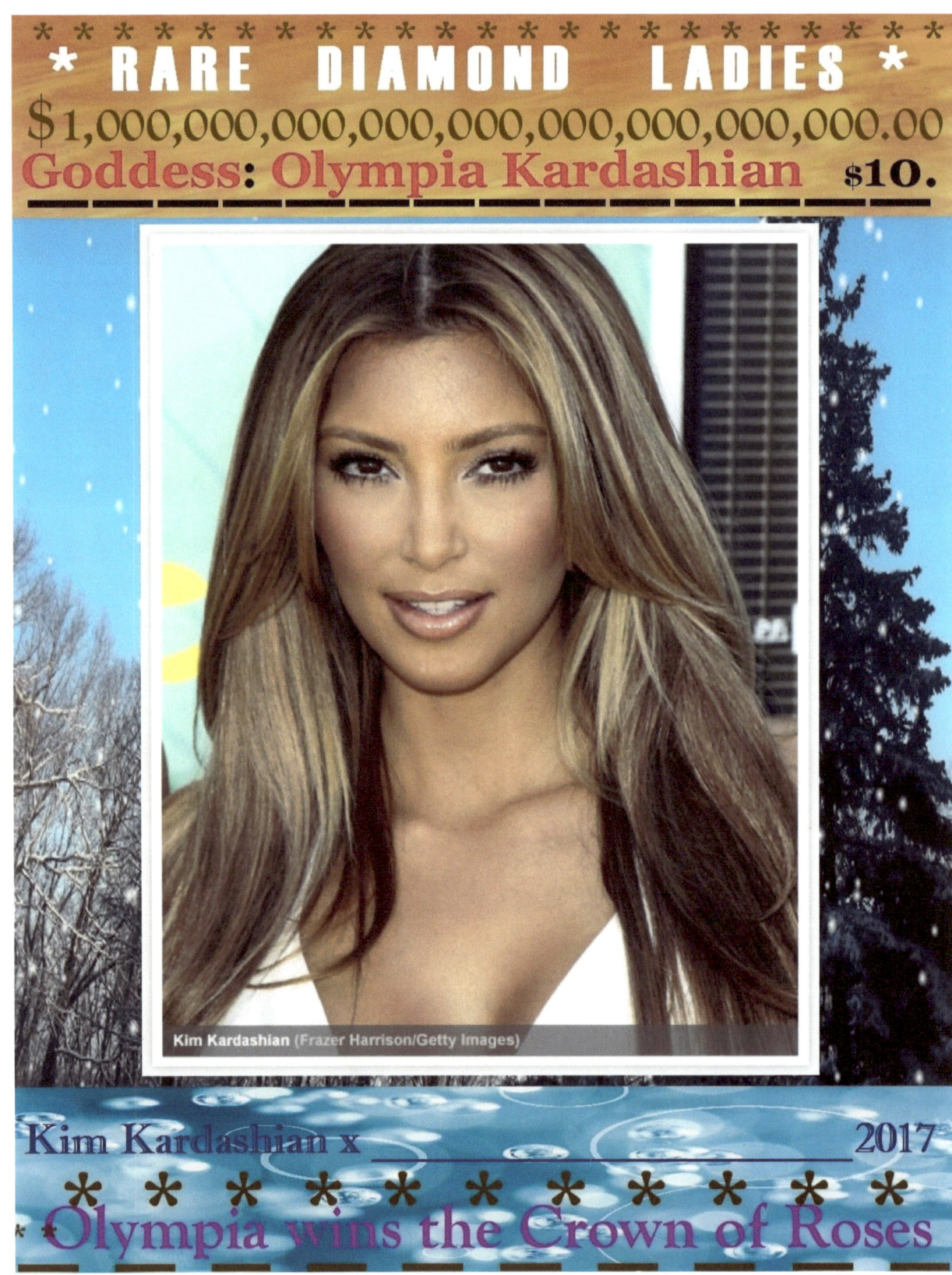

Kim Kardashian (Frazer Harrison/Getty Images)

Kim Kardashian x _____ 2017

* * * * * * * * * * * *
*Olympia wins the Crown of Roses

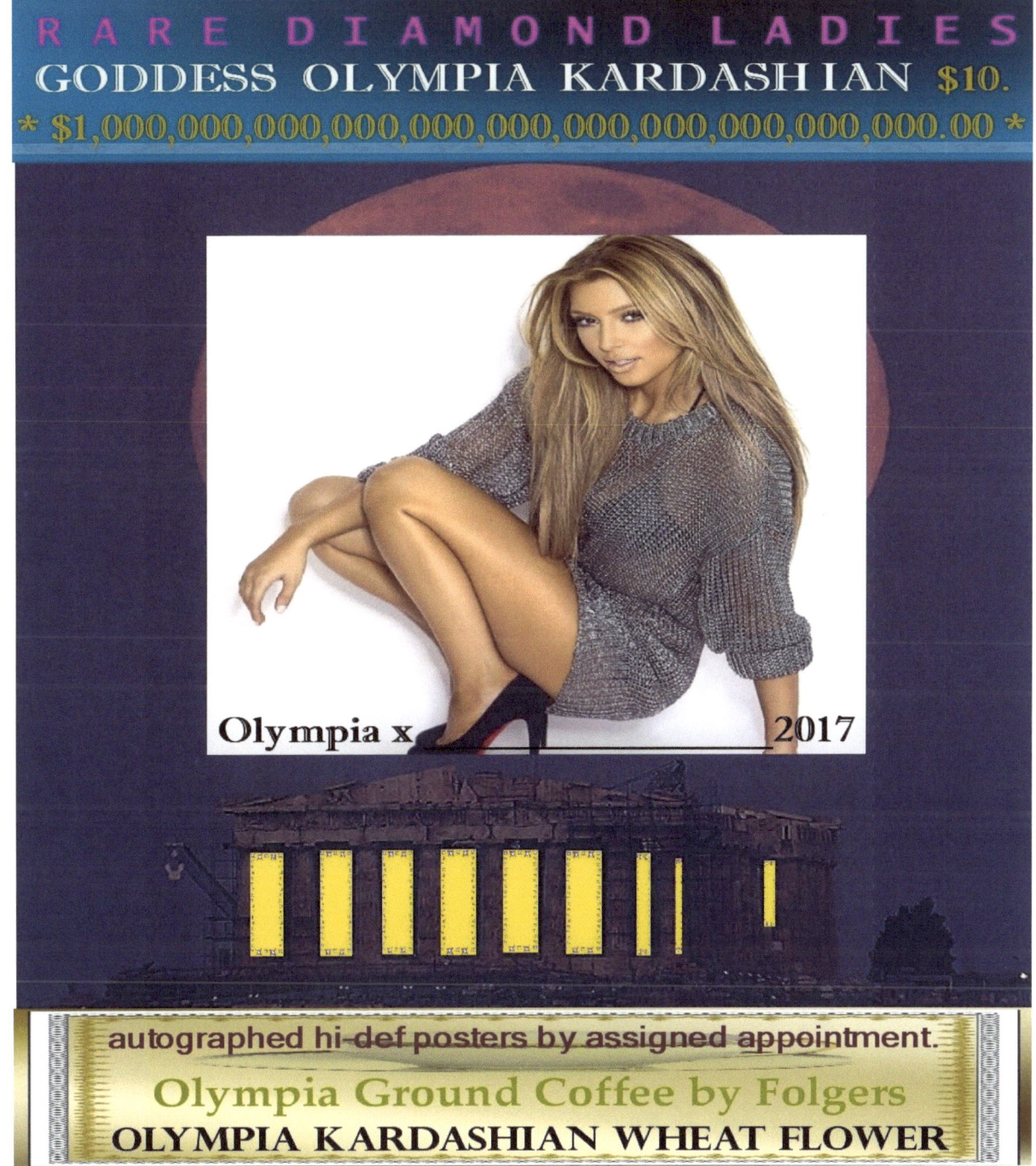

RARE DIAMOND LADIES

GODDESS OLYMPIA KARDASHIAN $10.

* $1,000,000,000,000,000,000,000,000,000,000,000.00 *

Olympia x   2017

autographed hi-def posters by assigned appointment.

Olympia Ground Coffee by Folgers

OLYMPIA KARDASHIAN WHEAT FLOWER

RARE DIAMOND LADIES

*   *

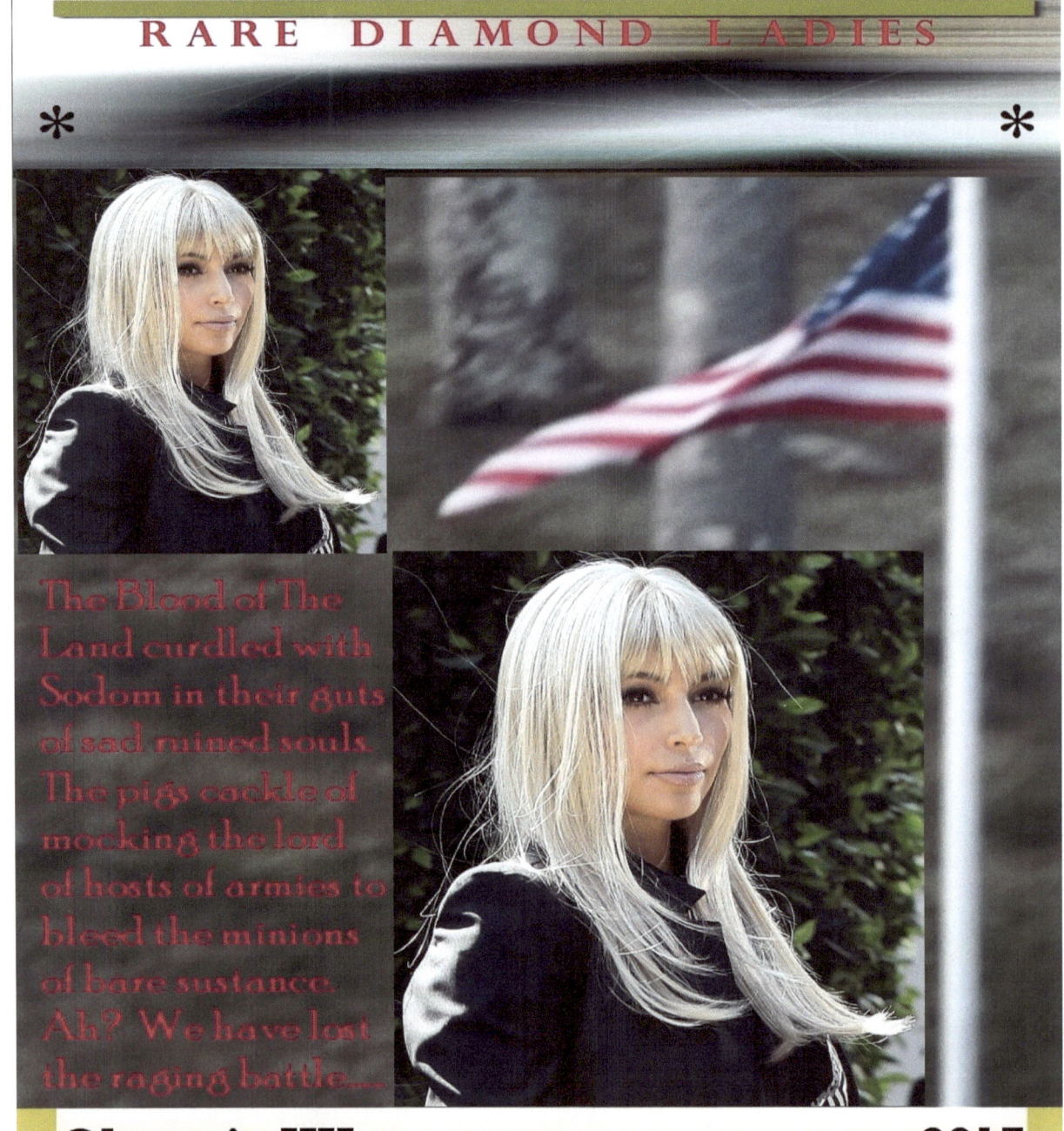

The Blood of The
Land curdled with
Sodom in their guts
of sad mined souls.
The pigs cackle of
mocking the lord
of hosts of armies to
bleed the minions
of bare sustance.
Ah? We have lost
the raging battle....

Olympia KK x_____**2017**

autographed hi-def posters cost many prayers.
beckon the lepers of hypocrisy to sorrow more.

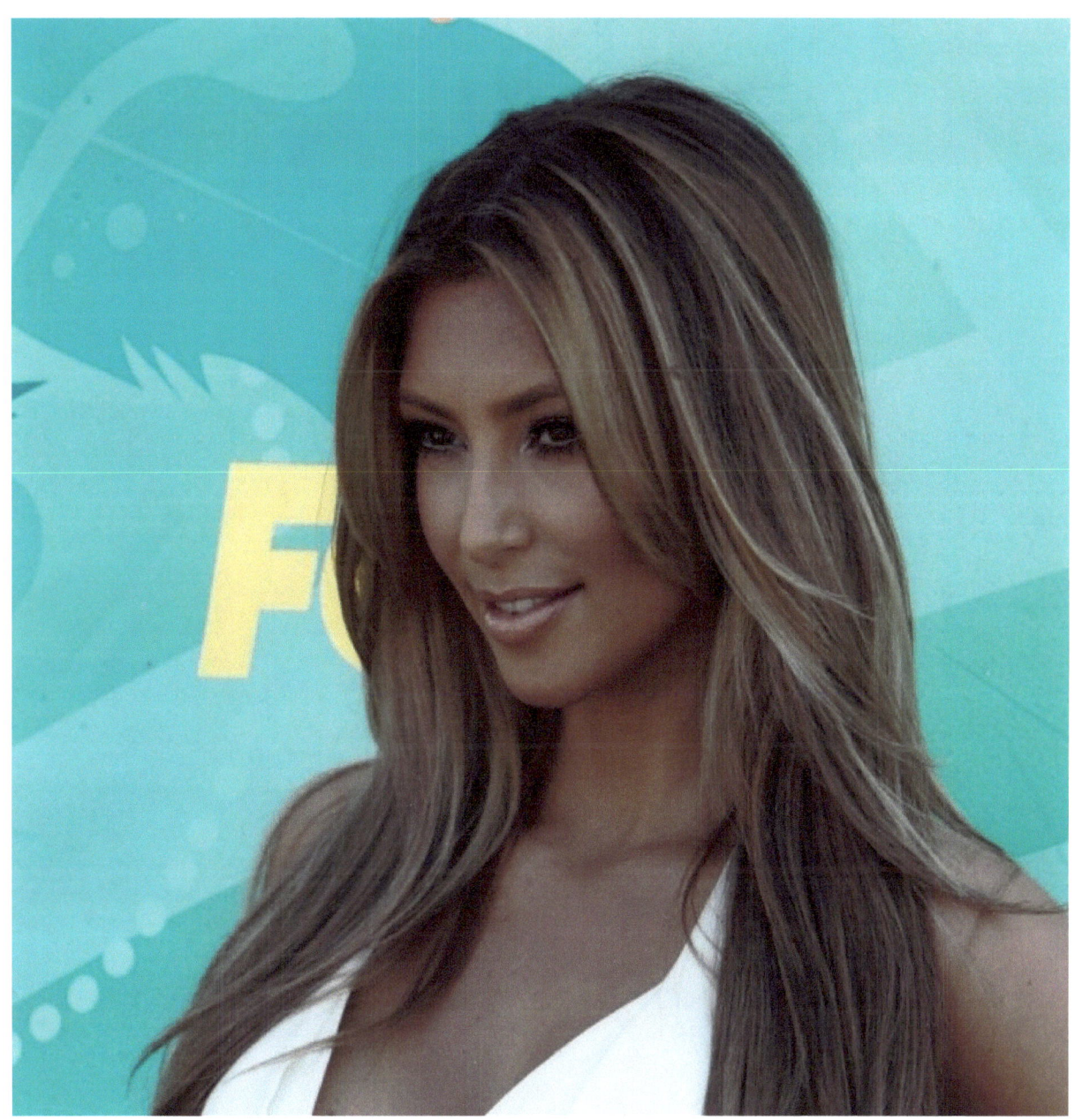

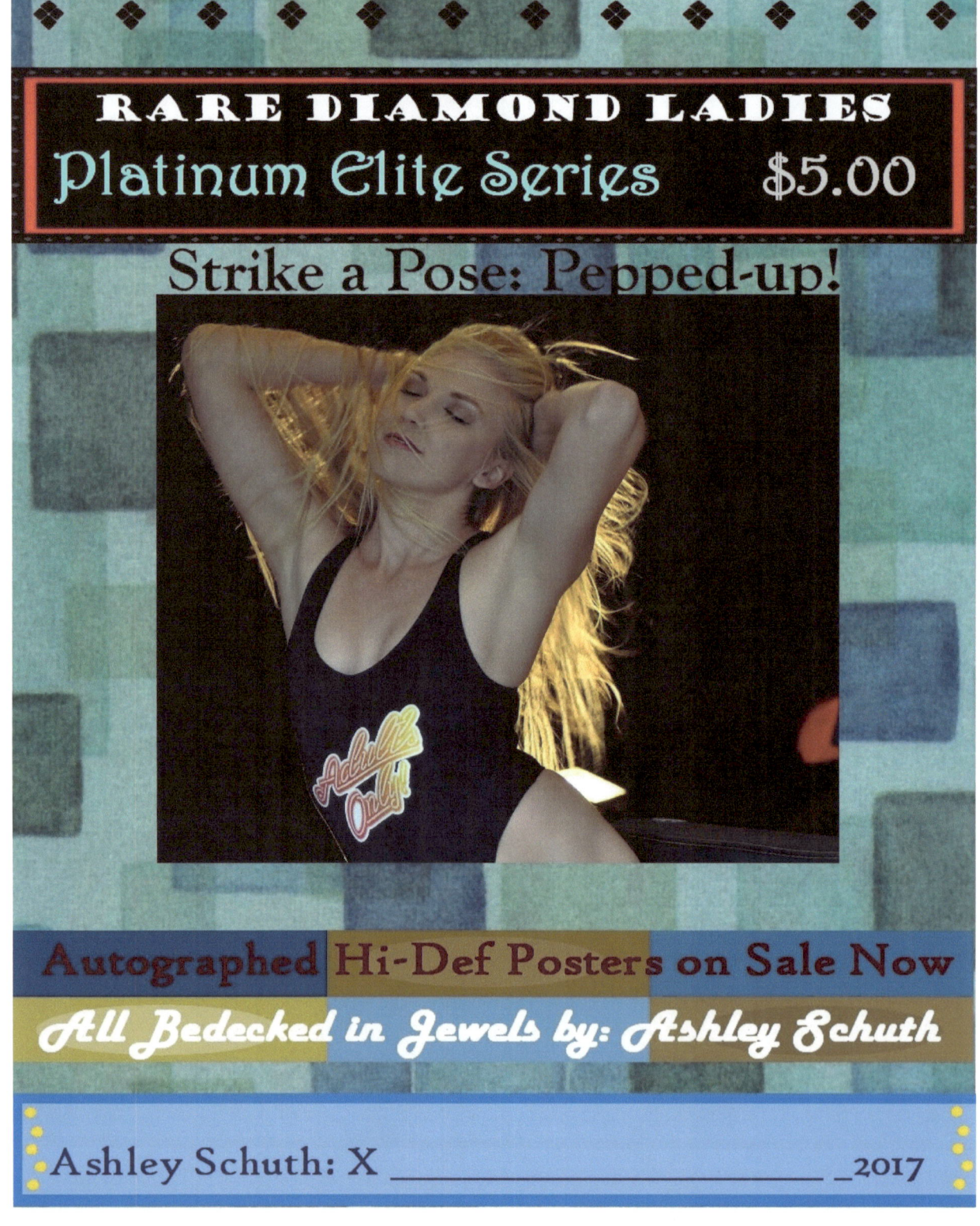

RARE DIAMOND LADIES
Platinum Series Edition: Portrait
$5.00

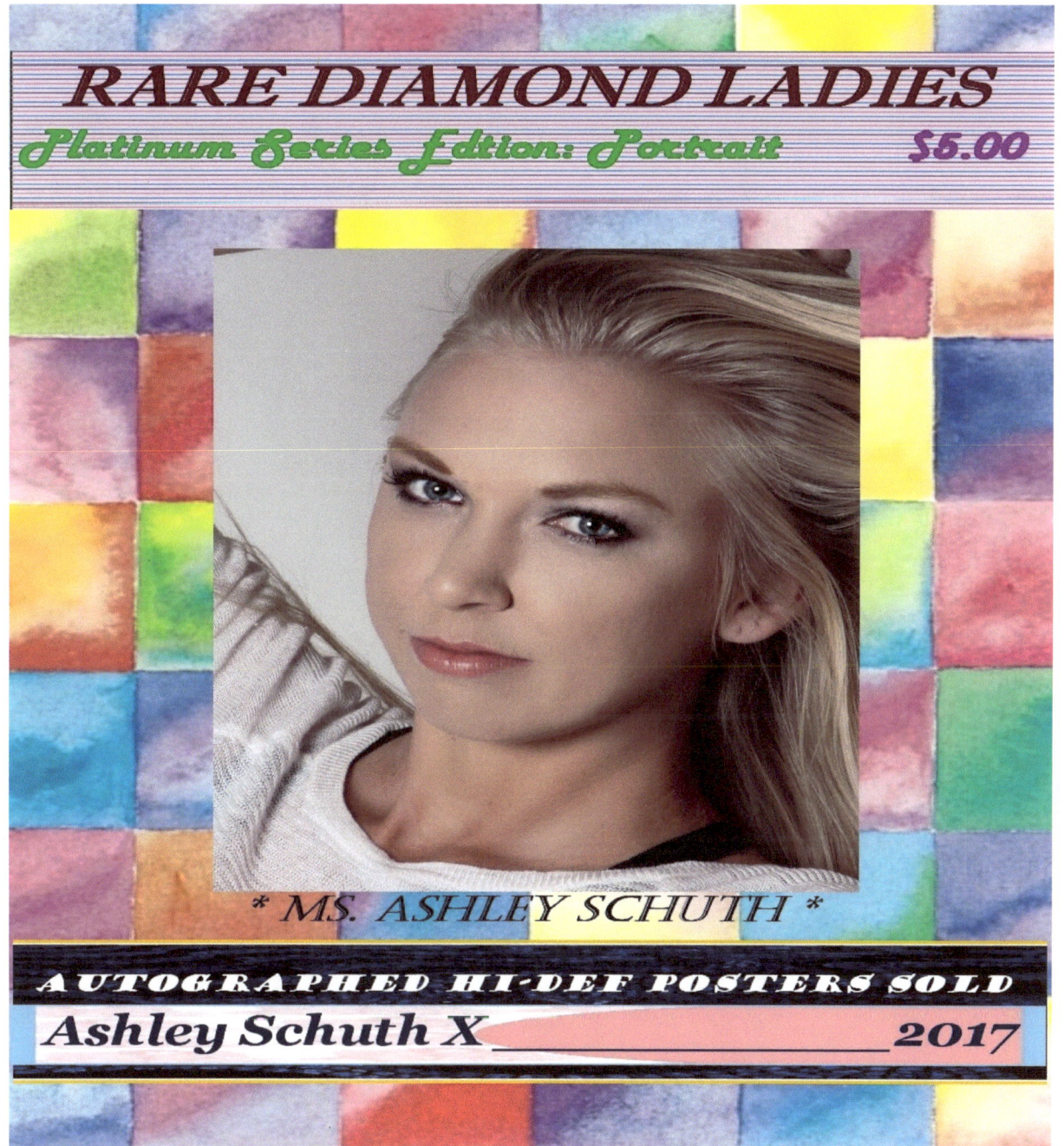

* MS. ASHLEY SCHUTH *

AUTOGRAPHED HI-DEF POSTERS SOLD

Ashley Schuth X_____ 2017

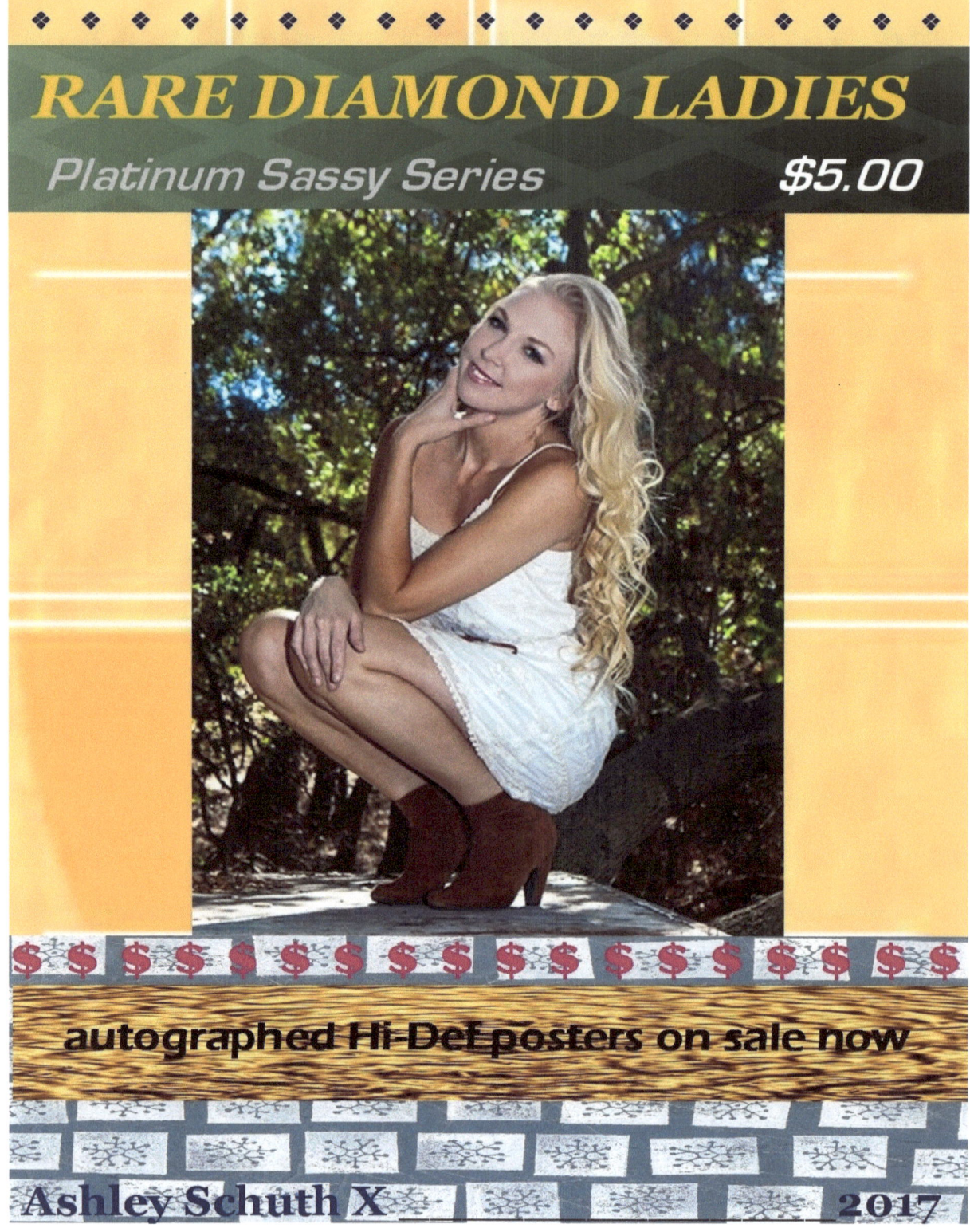

RARE DIAMOND LADIES

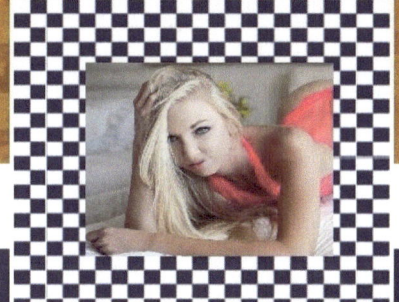

Platinum Series $5.00

An Ashley Schuth Enterprise

"Imagine your her lover"

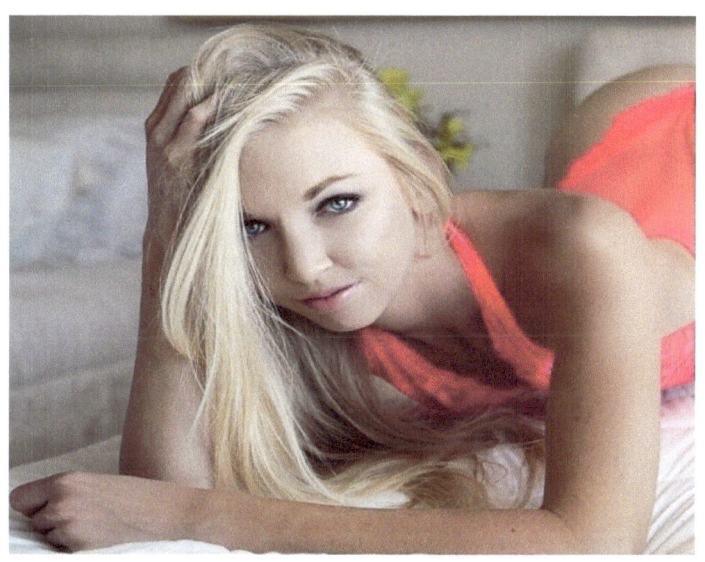

Autographed Hi-Def Posters Sold Now

Copyrighted to: Ashley Schuth Company

Ashley Schuth X _____ 2017

RARE DIAMOND LADIES

Platinum Series Edition $5.00

Ashley Schuth

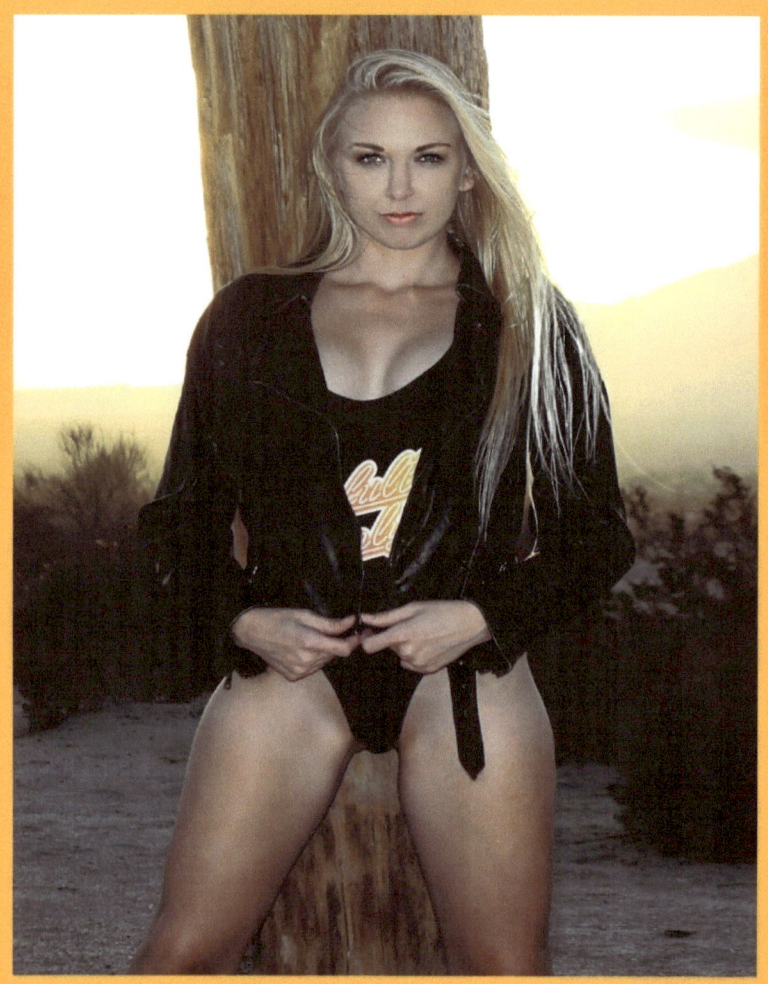

autographed hi-def posters on sale now

Copyright: Ashley Schuth on Fire

Scripted X_____ 2017

Ashley Schuth: "The Mystical Trance" INC.

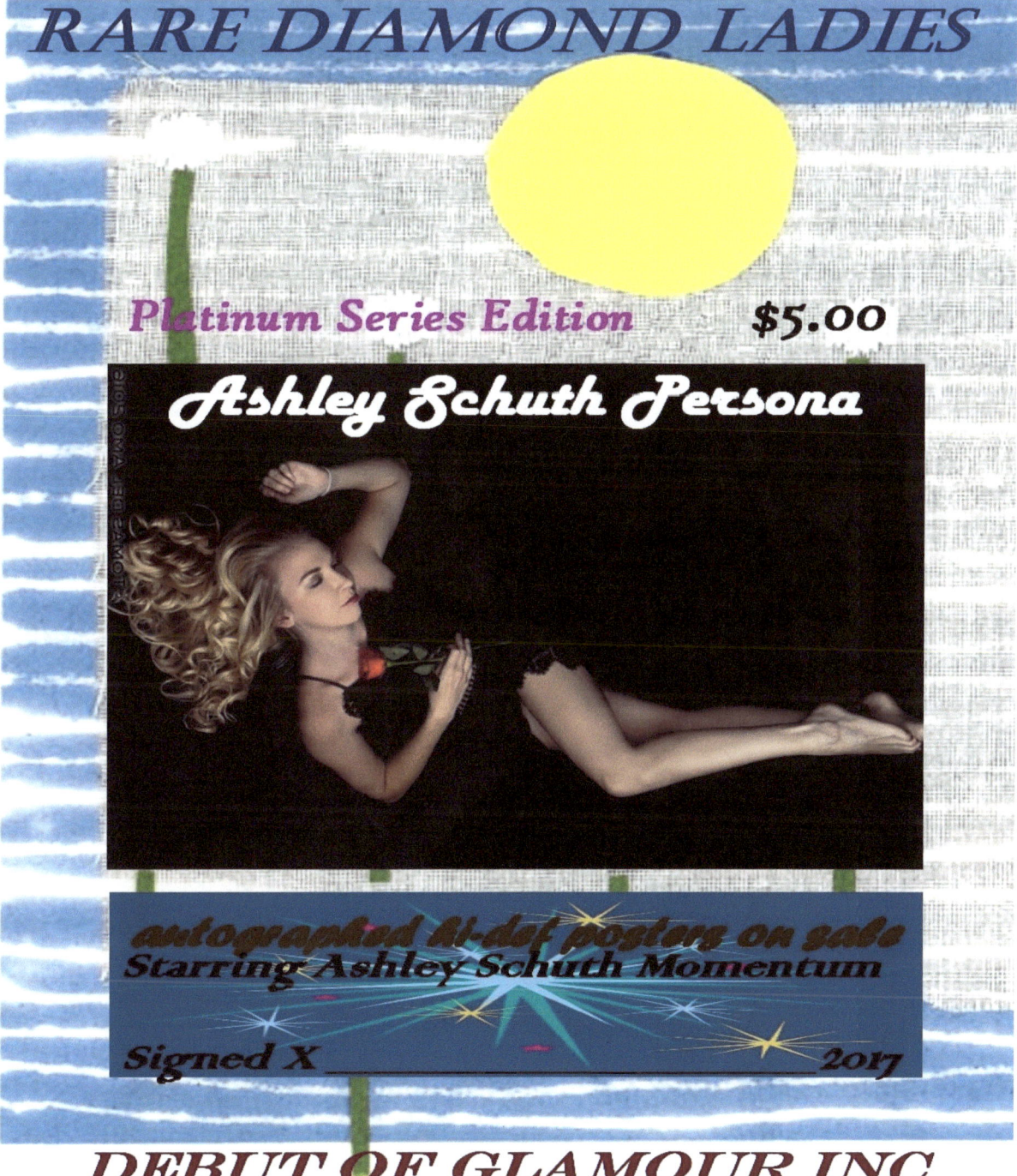

Rare Diamond Ladies

Platinum Series Edition $5.00

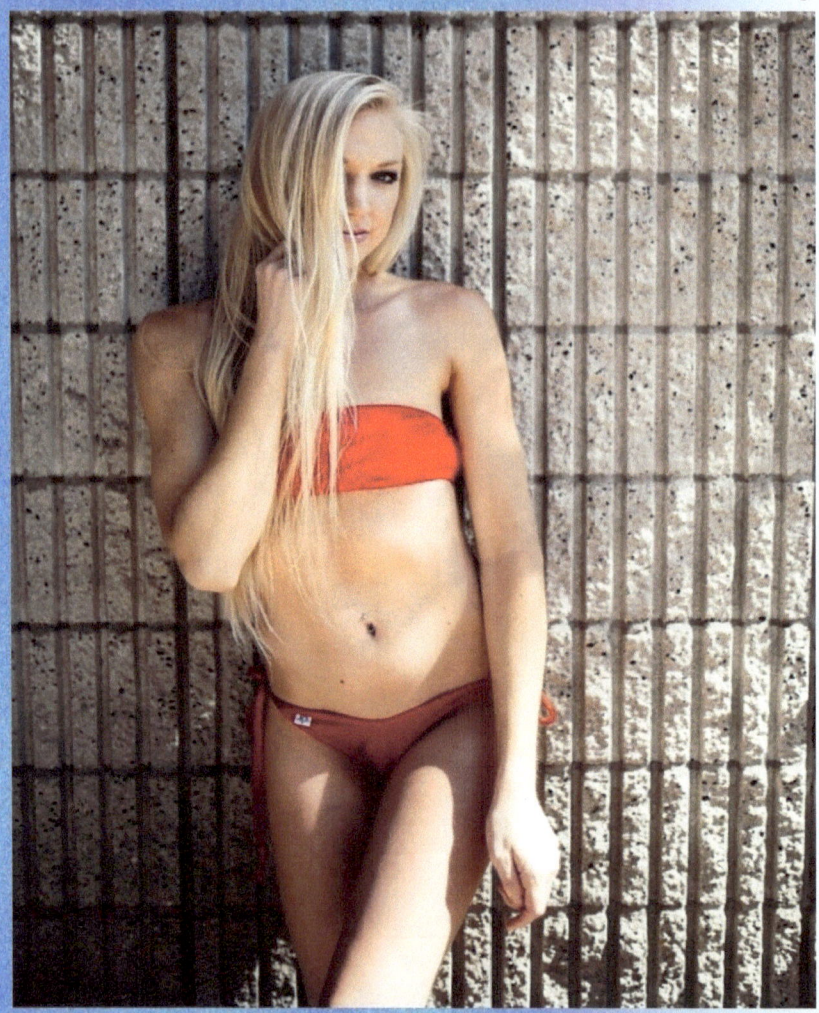

Autographed Hi-Def Posters on Sale Now

Ashley Schuth X

2017

Rare Diamond Ladies

Platinum Series Edition $5.00

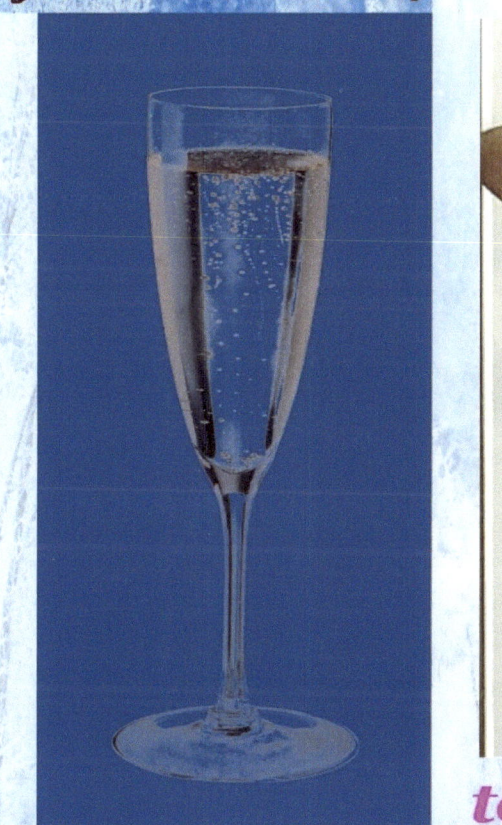

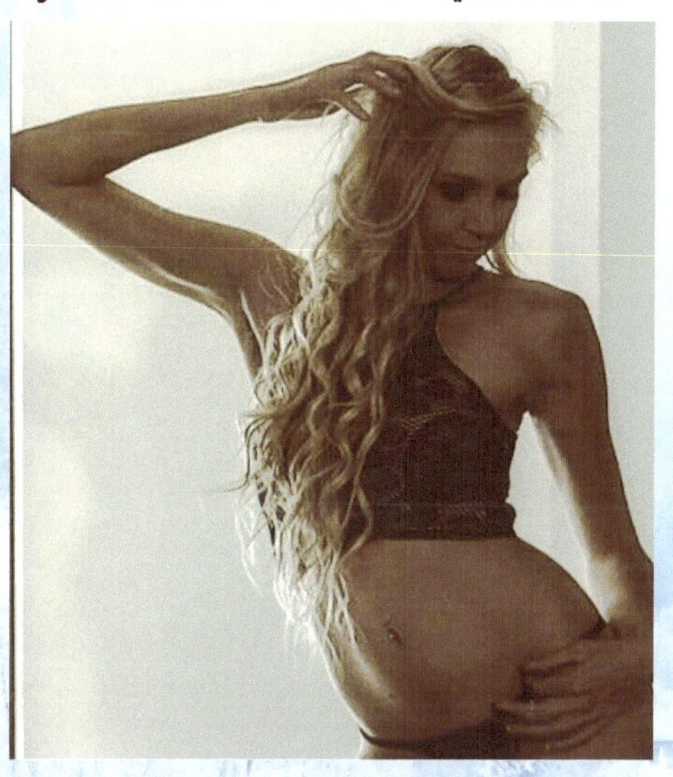

touched by treasure

autographed hi-def poster sales

Ashley Schuth: Goddess of Wine

Ashley Schuth X _____ *2017*

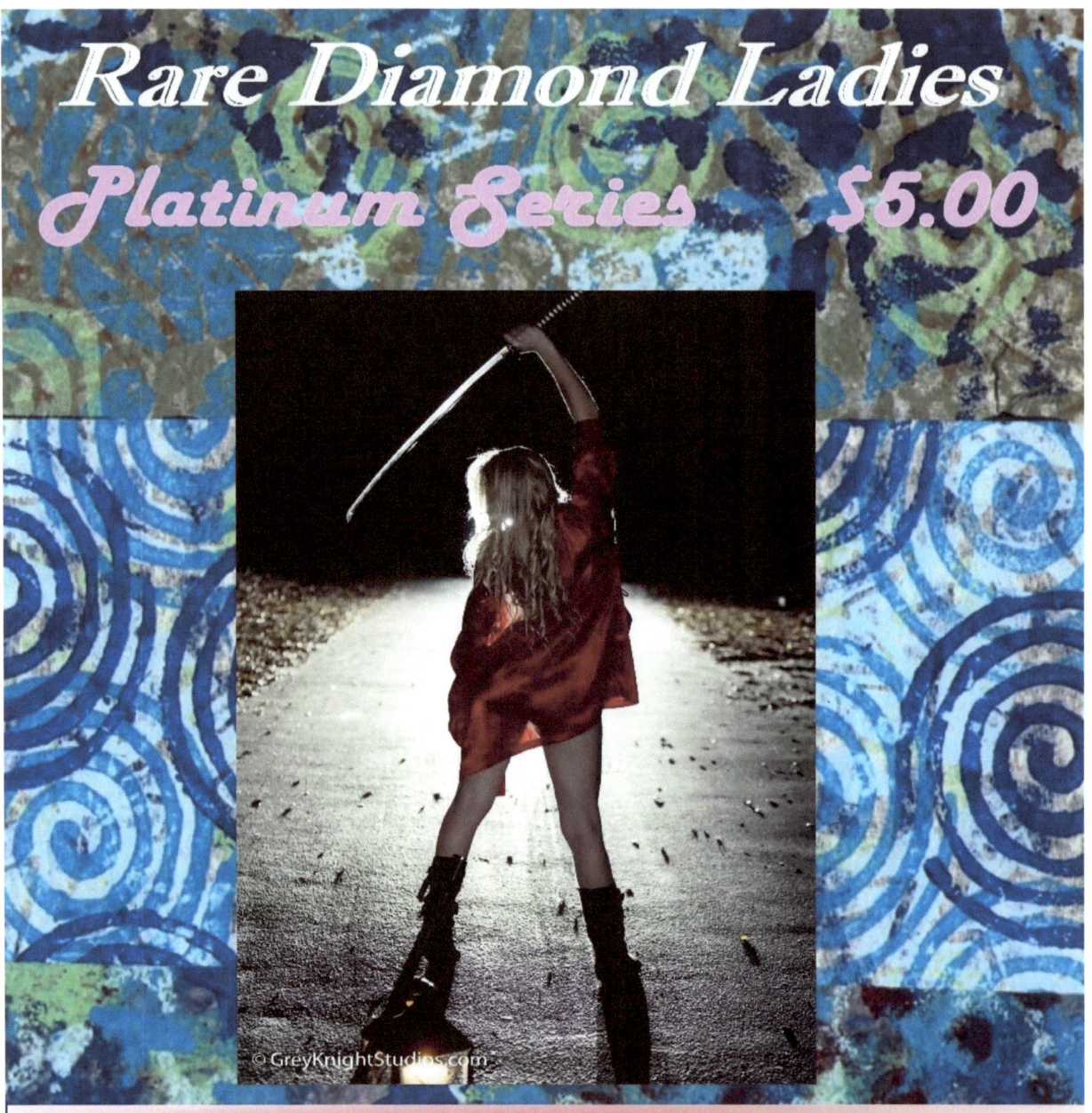

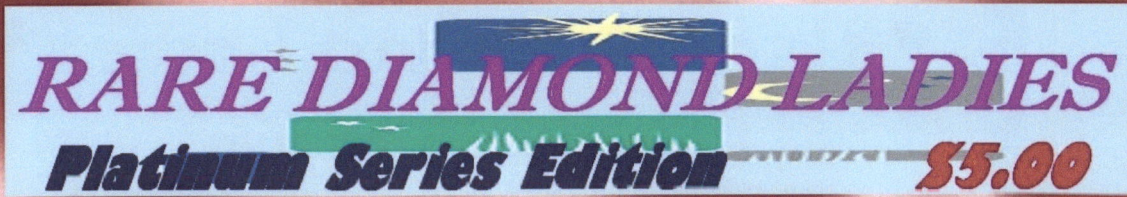

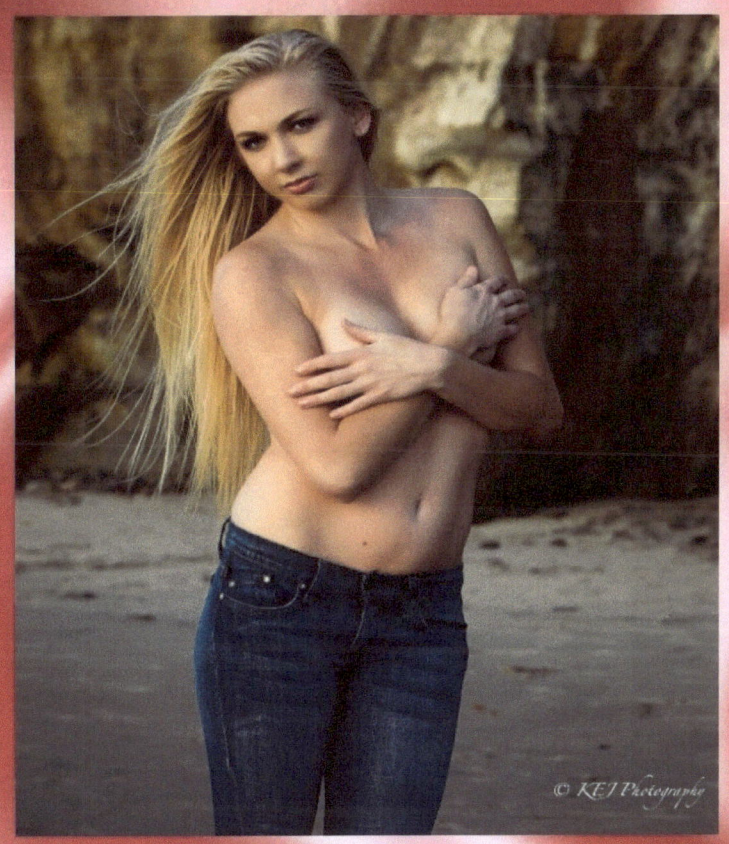

Autographed Hi-Def Posters on Sale Now

Ashley Schuth X_____2017
Cute and Sexy Lingerie by A.S. Dreamwear

* Rare Diamond Ladies *

Platinum Series Elite Edition $5.00

Special Ashley Schuth: "Naughty Nighty"

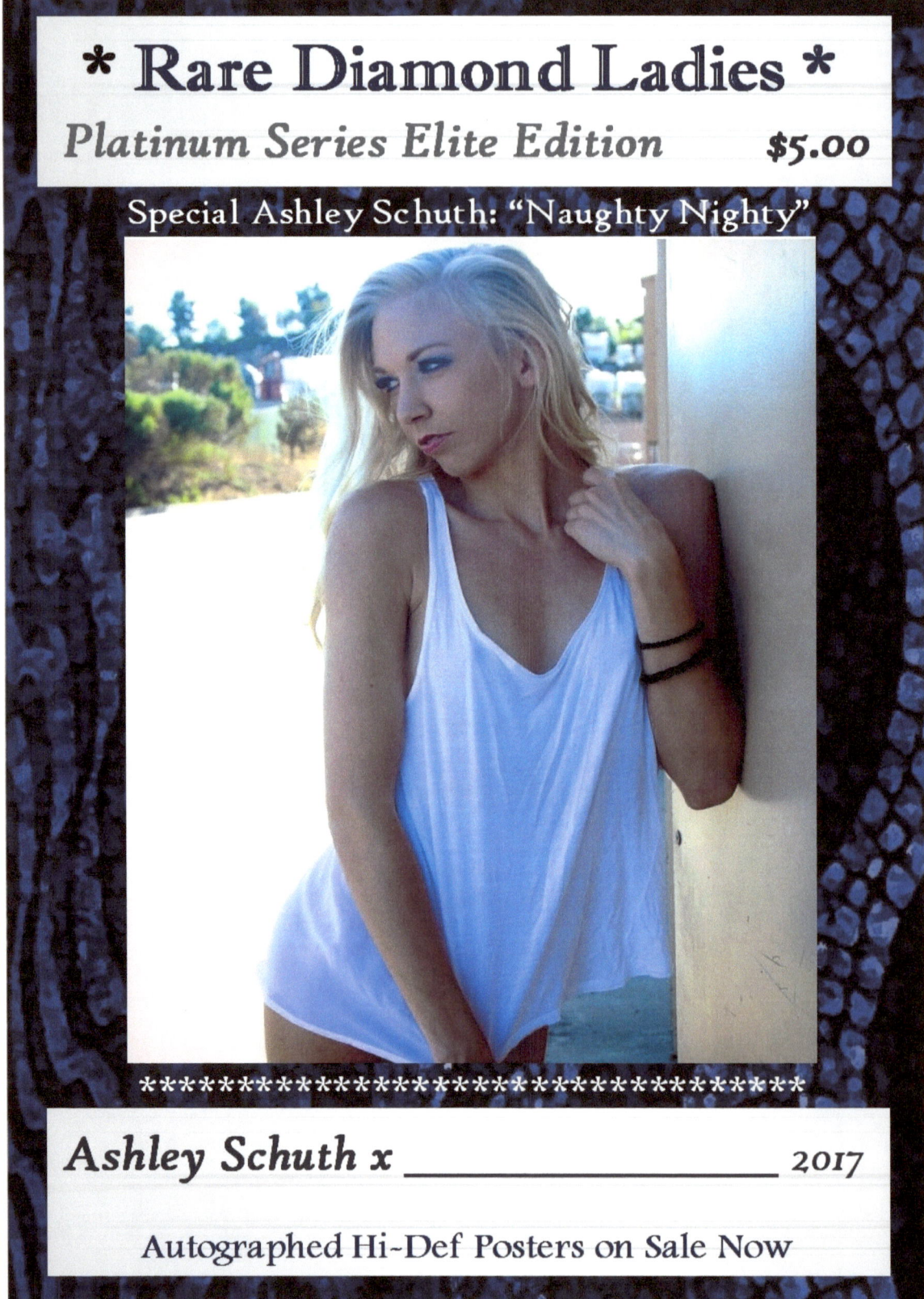

****

Ashley Schuth x _____ *2017*

Autographed Hi-Def Posters on Sale Now

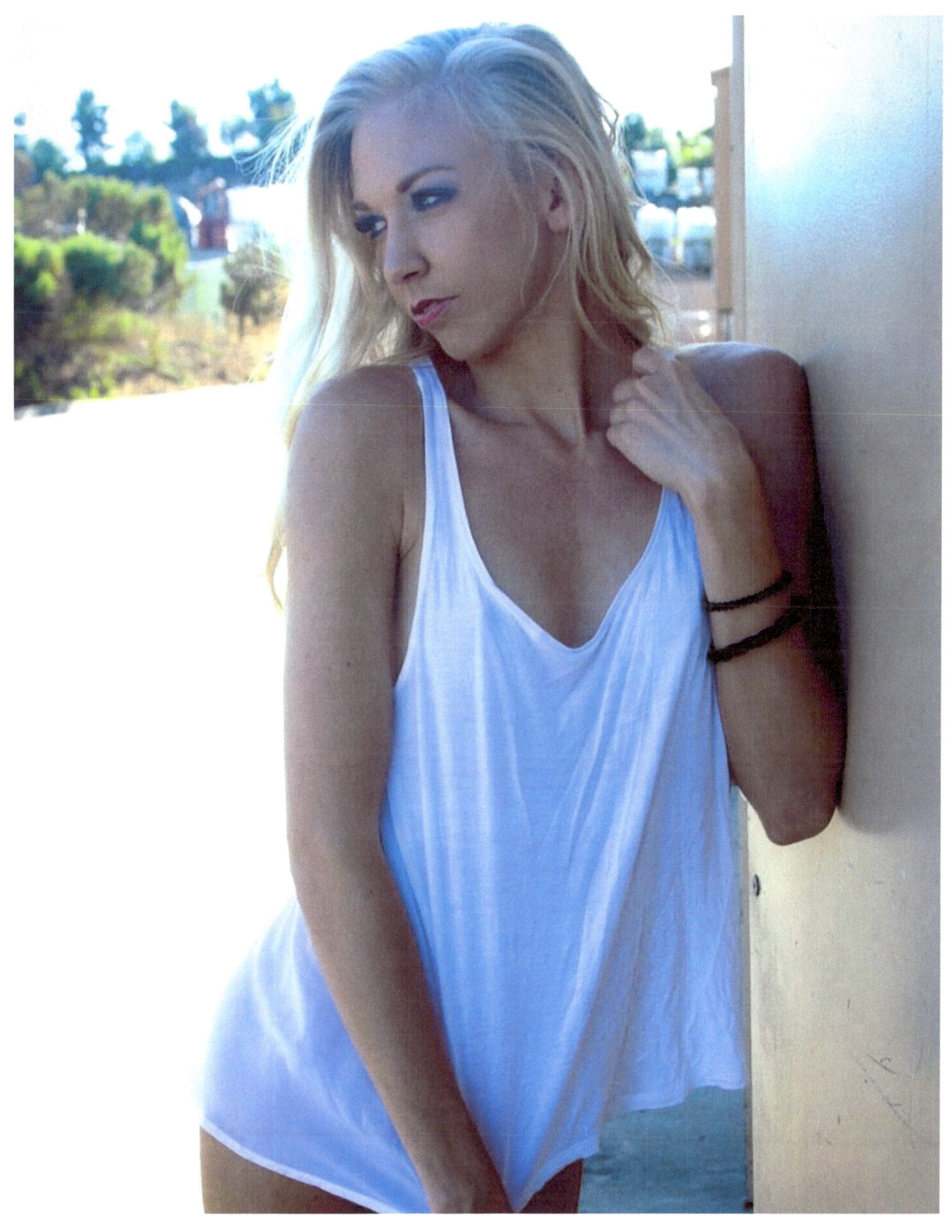

The reiterated conclusion of $40.00 USD an hour, is that this must be a global plan. I repeat the formula of the $2,000.00 dollar Homestead. We first buy one acre of rural property on a wooded lot at the average rate of $1,000.00 an acre. This will alleviate the quick concern of our returning soldiers and other youthful men from thee old Act of 20 acres for $25.00 USD. Now that we have the wooded lot we invest in a chain saw and weed through the scrub wood and sell some of the scrub wood for about $2,000.00 bucks. Leaving the new sum of $2,000.00 dolaros to repay us for the original $1000 dollars invested and giving us enough to buy a fairly new trailer home @ $1,000.00 remodeled. Now we own the property and own the mobile home. There are four other investments to capstone the comfort of home.... one is solar panels on the roof of the trailer, second is a satellite dish, third is a artisan well, and fourth is a Sheepherder Wood / Coal cook stove. Maybe we need to sell more scrub wood, instead of buying things used at sales. Our next investment will be a 30 foot Mess Tent from wholesalers and plant that on one of the four corners of the property, this is for summertime living and creating straight-wood lumber in the Winter months with a felt lining and two canister wood stoves. The lumber will be used in the Spring for building a log cabin in a third corner of the lot. More of the remaining lumber will be used in building a Saltbox home as our showpiece for the property... good to find land with wildlife on the parcel, but as forestry dissipates... since we are rural we can raise small livestock and milk and eggs and gardening as well. Hope you are earning money on your computer now and can afford a foundation for your home and other amenities that come with the average home... documents like this are good, as are photographs and arts and crafts. This $2,000 dollar program seems more expensive... but remember the straight wood also has branches that make quick sales in firewood.
The forty dollars an hour will come... benefits as veterans or other recipients should make it easy to jockey (we can have horses too) about till the flow is liquid and your assets have already just increased too $300,000.00. Not bad at all for a few years of tinkering.

Global Imperialism...
Brought to you by:
pmpbroadcasting@outlook.com,
Signed:
David M Pedjoe

Dear Fellow Citizens of the Globe:

I prayed to God a few years ago in the shower and asked Him to give the World a blessing you could not contain and on two counts He gave you this blessing already and one was through His only begotten Son: Lord Jesus. You don't believe me then try to contain it. Thee other, at least on my count, and - I reiterate for the last time! Was the $10 Million USD equation by which I calculated to all of you, how to go about the process of pseudo debonair and debutante at 16 years of age and the cyclical fact of "God's Portion" aka: a real piece of the pie... and it went like this: when a lovely couple reaches 16 years of age, "evenly-yoked" that together they receive a stipend of $10 Million dollars... In certain factions of fear (not of the Lord) but of terrorism (war) and natural disasters like tornados the lovely couple build a Ollie North fortress (as a house built on a rock) that with all the horns and whistles of safety and security costs the young generation about $1 Million dollars to make manifest and are left with $9 Million USD or other global currency. From there they basically have some income for food and travel, it only costs about $10,000.00 dollars to tour around the World and steeply $50,000.00 for gourmet food (consult your nutritionist) leaving in interest of $Nine Million at about 5% thee old standard with six percent for global entrepreneurial investments, and earn $450 Thousand a year minus food and travel. Within a few years the couple's income reaches $11 Million Dollars and the rule is to donate that One Million above legal standard as a donation to their community for I'll say a Hockey Rink. From there the lovely generations of couples garner in goods as collectibles as said to be eccentric but is really eclectic and within a few years of collecting antique guns and silver spoons - the hobby gets old and the unit build a community Museum to house their collections and can even have the hockey rink and museum in their household name. Now God's Will is Done and the couple can dabble in many legal areas of life and God's Kingdom on Earth. This said and done: each time the loving couple reaches the $11 Million dollar mark again, the One Million goes back into the "kitty" for future debonair and debutante couples to repeat the process with a $10 Million Dollar stipend. So basically the entire Globe is born with $10 Million Dollars and dies with Ten Million, after not actually spending a dime. This money is put back into the Treasury backed by an undisclosed amount of gold and national archives for the continuum of the $10,000,000.00 Dollar Family. Here is the second blessing the World cannot contain. Praise The Lord. Accept this strategy. Amen

David Pedjoe
http://www.zhibit.org/artlink

Dear Super Models:

I have interest once again to reiterate your plans to hold out on nudity, for as long as you can, but certainly before your wallowing in the mire. Being put out to pasture, was a warning my (passed-on) Mom... taught me about to save you girls from rainy-days. My Dad and John Robert Powers Modeling Agency had nothing to do with me as an artisan / photographer. Well there were assets donated to me, by Dad... and once he said your family is with you in spirit. I noted Jacqueline Bouvier was once a JRP girl and models were paid $2,000.00 a shoot. I also offered scholarships to JRP on mine own... so Dad wouldn't go to hell. The payment agreement I read and knew about some twice 90 day deal, that added up to six months before granted payment. But Mom was also a model of wigs and an off-Broadway actress, had me in youth... try out for: "South Pacific" and Ms. Clifford had me as the King in "The Tax King" Play. As I was dressed up a English Lord in a long red jacket and ruffled black shorts and black tights: "I am your King" and vowed to pay you back! This is just a synapsis of my life that led to esteem your progress as I calculated the persona you could attain. It began with "Pink" and the backstage "meet and greet" for $75,000.00 dollars, when the greats only got $20,000.00 for a three day layover in on average NY. NY. and Los Angelus. That dude wasn't driving modeling careers to obsolete annihilation. Therefore I intervened. First with Paula Jones and a $ Million USD kiss. Then I calculated the real results of... what I say again? Well actually it's more than just nudity... it's a three hundred photograph shoot = I can handle 800 photos on my 4 GB San Disk and take the shoot in one day via Jet Blue to Worcester MA. 01602 USA. I will arrange airfare and Hong Kong attire and I'll keep a copy of the photos, only allowing me to create photo story 3 videos with, that I email to you anyways. But you keep the clothes, the camera and the San Disk... then we would allocate the photos into high-definition prints @ $ 3000.00 USD per print, created by publisher and earning income of prints x 800 I would hope. Then being famous (without nudity) you would earn through saturation marketing, as onto Picasso or the price of $ 100,000.00 USD per personally autographed pictures, in an unlimited series, as unto the Farrah Fawcett "pink" bath-suit. That mistakenly had a stamped on signature... that ruined her famed value. Now you know. This should not happen to you. You have evolved as a model, and in demand... as wolves hunger for your, in the buff; composure... still not attained and need it not. The tease, creates a challenge and your haunted by chump-change porn images that disgust you. But if you did, the likes of Esquire your nudity would fetch $ One Billion Dollars! How? Do you know how many magazines would sell? You did the David and Jesus trick? The advertisers would pay big bucks for image in the pages of High-end Markets. You get the copyrights to the image and sell ads and rake in $ One Billion USD for just a few of the business hook-biters. Never mind the magazine itself, and the fact you sold all thee advertisements. Models comprehend this as well as you gentlemen of agreement. Congratulations... your now valued in assets near Two Billion USD. Here's an easy $ 2 Billion for Vanessa Williams = a rebel of tradition. Instant Fame! Instant Gratuities! Fiat!

David M Pedjoe

Envision yourself on my portico, as we indulge with ice tea and caviar with toast triangles and farmers chess. It is a warm and breezy starlit night. You look dazzling in your refined attire, an artist's dream? I smile upon you and gaze to hearts content, with no lust in mine being. Such is the beauty of youth, the becoming sensation of my portraiture. I place in your hand a sparkling diamond as a token of appreciation. The night lingers on with laughter and patiently we prepare each and other for the studio, where I will paint you.

The time has come, we retreat into my living quarters, not holding hands or making goo-goo eyes upon you. This is professional business ethics, with none but the Masters brushes to capture you on canvas. You prepare to pose in elegant lingerie, my stamina increases to do a perfect masterpiece. You are on a tufted bed of navy blue velour and golden pillows. You relax and our company is no longer, that of a stranger. The room is scented by your perfume, your bath robe hangs on the bed post. I see you clearly now and we whisper as the brushstrokes wet the gesso on the canvas panel. You yawn and grow weary... I say: do not be afraid, there is none crime, when I am a knight and protector. You dose off, as I concentrate mine Merlin magic. The night will fulfill your dreams as I create the mightiness of your image, through the deed I am gifted with. Paint is mixed and colors flow, I do not intend to copy your attire and improvise with mine own designer wear. I see the impression, then again I challenge myself to fine art with acrylics. The sky begins to lighten and it is finished.

You awaken with no disturbances and I say good morning. Surprising you with sparkling champagne with a rose in the flute. Voila, I claim and show you the portrait. It is yours to keep with copyrights included. You moan and smile with awe. Compliment me as a gentleman. Hoping we could celebrate this way once again. I bow slightly and proclaim: "It would be my pleasure, young lady." A drug and alcohol-free meeting of creation. A perfect lady and a perfect gentleman. Who would disagree? Why? Jealousy: which is a sin to man. Beware of saboteurs. The diamond sparkles!

Wrought of you by:
David Pedjoe